Positive thinking is the key which unlocks the doors of the world.

— Samuel McChord Crothers

A Daybook of

Positive Thinking

Daily Affirmations of Gratitude and Happiness

A Blue Mountain Arts® Collection

Edited by Patricia Wayant

Blue Mountain Press™

Boulder, Colorado

Library of Congress Control Number: 2011910378
ISBN: 978-1-59842-604-5

▉ and Blue Mountain Press are registered in U.S. Patent and Trademark Office.
Certain trademarks are used under license.

Printed in China.
Sixth Printing: 2014

Blue Mountain Arts, Inc.

P.O. Box 4549, Boulder, Colorado 80306

Contents

Be Positive...
Be Happy

Refuse to be unhappy;
   be cheerful instead.
Refuse to let your troubles multiply;
   just take them one by one.
Refuse to complain about things;
   learn to improve your surroundings
and create your world
   the way you believe it should be.

Refuse to dwell on the mistakes
    or disappointments
that are sometimes a part of life;
instead learn how you can
    make things better.
Be optimistic.
Be energetic and positive
    about the things you do,
and always hope for the best.
Believe in yourself at all times
    and in all aspects of your life.
Before you know it,
those wonderful dreams
you have believed in all your life
    will come true,
and your life will be
the happy and successful life
    that it was meant to be.

— Ben Daniels

Reach for the Good

There is good in life every day.
Take a few minutes to distract yourself
from your concerns —
long enough to draw strength from a tree
or to find pleasure in a bird's song.
Return a smile;
realize that life is a series of levels,
cycles of ups and downs —
some easy, some challenging.

Through it all, you will learn;
you will grow strong in faith;
you will mature in understanding.
The difficult times are often
the best teachers, and there is
good to be found in all situations.
Reach for the good.
Be positive, and don't give up.

— Pamela Owens Renfro

Life Is Everything You Make It... and More

In life, there will inevitably be obstacles to encounter. But don't worry that they will seem too great for you to handle, because you can. You may doubt yourself at times, but know that if you have faith, you have everything. Faith is the key to being successful.

If you know you are capable of anything because of who you are, you will always reach your destination. It may not always be easy, but it will always be worth it. Look ahead of you, never behind. Have faith in yourself. If you do, you will be amazed at what you can accomplish.

— T. L. Nash

Find Something Every Day to Be Positive About

Every day, be full of awareness
    of the beauty around you.
Be full of gratitude
    for friends and family,
for the goodness you find in others,
for your health and all you're capable of.
Be full of acceptance
    of yourself and others —
without conditions or judging,
knowing that differences and changes
    make life interesting.
Appreciate the gifts of laughter
    and fun in your life,
and find contentment in knowing
    that you can always control
your ability to look on the bright side.

— Barbara Cage

Promise yourself
to accept life as it comes
and truly make each day special —
to become more independent
and more willing to change —
to fill your life
with special times,
and make your dreams come true.

— Deanna Beisser

Choose Your Thoughts Wisely

Accept and appreciate that you're the one most responsible for making your dreams come true. Be your own best friend. Cheer yourself on.

Choose your thoughts, because if you don't, you're still making a choice and you'll have to take what you get. In your mind's eye, create a positive picture that will draw what you want to you. Your intuition is powerful; use it. Keep your desires burning. Don't be afraid to take careful chances.

Inform yourself. Make the connection between your thoughts, your actions, and the results you're getting. The cumulative quality of your actions will weave the tapestry of your destiny. Live your life consciously; don't just let your life live you.

Look at your circumstances as life lessons rather than adversities. Keep a careful watch over your joy. Cherish it. Acknowledge your blessings, no matter how small they may seem. You are a student in the school of life and in many ways your own teacher. Appreciate the lessons you've learned, and enjoy life, others, and yourself.

— Donna Fargo

Positive Thinkers Have Twelve Qualities in Common

They have confidence in themselves

They have a very strong sense of purpose

They never have excuses for not doing something

They always try their hardest for perfection

They never consider the idea of failing

They work extremely hard toward their goals

They know who they are

They understand their weaknesses as well as
	their strong points

They can accept and benefit from criticism

They know when to defend what they are doing

They are creative

They are not afraid to be a little different in
	finding innovative solutions that will enable
	them to achieve their dreams

— Susan Polis Schutz

To Live a Positive Life Is...

To live your life with no regrets...

To reach for a dream
and make it your own...

To be brave enough
to invest a part of your heart
in something real that brings you
great pleasure...

To have a close circle of friends
and the love of family to share
all of life's special moments with...

To have a special sense of purpose
and an inner strength
that gives you the confidence
to face each new day
with a positive attitude.

— Cindy Chuksudoon

Appreciate Your Own Greatness

Celebrate all you are
and how much you are loved.
Honor the person you are
and all you're becoming.
Be reminded of how many people
look up to you and admire
all the goodness in your heart.
Reach out and feel the happiness
others wish for you.
Do the things
that bring sunlight to your heart
and add a touch of magic to your dreams.

— Linda E. Knight

You may not understand
just how much your life means
to those around you —
how their days are brighter
    because you're here
and how the sound of your laughter
touches the heart of everyone
    around you.

Your presence adds something special
    and invaluable to the world.
You bring joy to those who love you
and a smile to everyone you meet.

Your life is a gift that is treasured.

— Star Nakamoto

Be as Happy as You Can Possibly Be

Release the child within you
so you can sing, laugh, and play.
List the things that you do best,
and give yourself a hug.
Accept compliments.
Dance barefoot.
Plan to fulfill a secret wish.
Laugh at yourself.
And above all,
remember you are loved.

— Jacqueline Schiff

Find happiness in nature
in the beauty of a mountain
in the serenity of the sea
Find happiness in friendship
in the fun of doing things together
in the sharing and understanding
Find happiness in your family
in the stability of knowing
   that someone cares
in the strength of love and honesty
Find happiness in yourself
in your mind and body
in your values and achievements
Find happiness in
everything
you
do

— Susan Polis Schutz

Always Keep a Dream in Your Heart

If you have a dream, then — by all means —
   do what it takes to make it come true.
If you have a goal, make it something
   you strive to accomplish.
If you have a hope, then hope for it
   with all your heart.
                                    — Collin McCarty

Do what you love
Control your own life
Have imaginative, realistic dreams
Work hard
Make mistakes but learn from them
Believe in yourself but know your limitations
Ignore people who tell you that you can't
Plow through obstacles and failures
Try to turn your dreams into reality

— Susan Polis Schutz

Resolve to Be the Best You Can Be

The world is kind, and there will be more hands held out ready to help you up than there were ready to beat you down. Though you may be at the bottom of the ladder of health, morals, and fortune, you may climb to the very top before another new year, if you only believe you can and resolve your will.

— Ella Wheeler Wilcox

Don't ever forget that you are unique.
Be your best self
and not an imitation of someone else.
Find your strengths,
and use them in a positive way.
Don't listen to those
who question the choices you make.
Travel the road that you have chosen,
and don't look back with regret.
Remember that there is plenty of time
to travel another road —
    and still another —
in your journey through life.
Take the time to find the route
that is right for you.

— Jacqueline Schiff

Happiness Comes from Within

Happiness cannot come from without. It must come from within. It is not what we see and touch or that which others do for us which makes us happy; it is that which we think and feel and do, first for the other fellow and then for ourselves.

— Helen Keller

Whether we live in a forty-room mansion, surrounded by servants and wealth, or find it a struggle to manage the rent month to month, we have it within our power to be fully satisfied and live a life with true meaning.

— Regina Hill

Joy is not in things; it is in us.

— Richard Wagner

True happiness must come from within you.
You will find happiness by letting your
conscience guide you — listen to it; follow it.
Your conscience is the key to your happiness.

— Karen Poynter Taylor

Let Go
of the Past

We consume our tomorrows
fretting about our yesterdays.

— Persius

Don't let old mistakes or misfortunes hold you down: learn from them, forgive yourself — or others — and move on. Do not be bothered or discouraged by adversity. Instead, meet it as a challenge. Be empowered by the courage it takes you to overcome obstacles. Learn something new every day.

— Ashley Rice

No amount of straining, crying, or agonizing can remake one single day of the year that is past. But a little careful planning and thoughtful working out can make many glorious days in the future.

— Author Unknown

Transform Failure into Success!

Probably he who never made a mistake never made a discovery.

— Samuel Smiles

The glory is not in never failing, but in rising every time you fail.

— Chinese Proverb

I am not discouraged, because every wrong attempt discarded is another step forward.

— Thomas A. Edison

We learn wisdom from failure much more than from success.

— Samuel Smiles

The men who try to do something and fail are infinitely better than those who try to do nothing and succeed.

— Lloyd Jones

Make Each Day a New Beginning

Finish every day and be done with it. You have done what you could. Some blunders and absurdities no doubt crept in; forget them as soon as you can. Tomorrow is a new day; begin it well and serenely and with too high a spirit to be cumbered with your old nonsense. This day is all that is good and fair. It is too dear, with its hopes and invitations, to waste a moment on the yesterdays.

— Ralph Waldo Emerson

Every morning you are handed twenty-four golden hours. They are some of the few things in this world that you get free of charge. If you had all the money in the world, you couldn't buy an extra hour. What will you do with this priceless treasure?

— Author Unknown

Try to keep your soul young and vibrant all your days and to imagine always ...that life is only beginning.

— George Sand

Believe That You Can Do Anything, and You Will!

Imagine yourself to be the type of person you want to be, and then be it. You may have to let go of some bad habits and develop some more positive ones, but don't give up — for it is only in trying and persisting that dreams come true.

Expect changes to occur, and realize that the power to make those changes comes from within you. Your thoughts and actions, your choices and decisions, and the way you spend your time determine who you are and who you will become.

You are capable and worthy of being and doing anything. You just need the discipline and determination to see it through. It won't come instantly, and you may backslide from time to time, but don't let that deter you. Never give up.

Life is an ever-changing process, and nothing is final. Therefore, each moment and every new day is a chance to begin anew.

— Barbara Cage

Thought is the great builder in human life: it is the determining factor. Continually think thoughts that are good, and your life will show forth in goodness.... Think thoughts of love, and you will love and will be loved.

— Ralph Waldo Trine

The greatest discovery of my generation is that human beings can alter their lives by altering their attitudes.

— William James

There are no limitations in what you can do except the limitations in your own mind as to what you cannot do.

— Darwin P. Kingsley

There is nothing either good or bad, but thinking makes it so.

— William Shakespeare

Practice
Acceptance

Acceptance means that you
    can find the serenity within
to let go of the past
    with its mistakes and regrets,
move into the future
    with a new perspective,
and appreciate the opportunity
    to take a second chance.

Acceptance means you'll find security again
when difficult times come into your life,
and comfort to relieve any pain.
You'll find new dreams, fresh hopes,
    and forgiveness of the heart.

Acceptance does not mean that
you will always be perfect.
It simply means that you'll always
overcome imperfection.

Acceptance is the road to peace —
letting go of the worst,
holding on to the best,
and finding the hope inside
that continues throughout life.

Acceptance is the heart's best defense,
love's greatest asset, and the easiest way
to keep your thoughts positive.

— Regina Hill

Make Today a Positive Day!

Today...
If the sun shines bright enough
   to warm your soul,
strong enough to fill your spirit,
and deep enough to bless
   your heart —
then it's a positive day!

Today...
If love is the best gift of all
and every moment is
    a dream come true...
If the sky smiles down on you
and all you've done for others
comes back to bless you...
If you feel like the
    most loved person on earth...
then it's a positive day!

— Linda E. Knight

In the
Difficult Times,
Keep a Positive Attitude

There are times in life
when things are not perfect,
when problems seem to surround you.
As you look for a way through them,
it's important to keep
a positive attitude about your life
and where you are going.

When you are going through
a difficult time,
you may wonder if you're making
the right choices.
You may wonder about how things
will turn out
if you take a different road.
But you are a strong
and motivated individual
who will rise to meet
the challenges that face you.
You will get through
the difficult times.

— Beverly A. Chisley

Keep in mind at all times
that you are very capable
of dealing with any complications
that life has to offer
So
do whatever you must
feel whatever you must
and keep in mind at all times
that we all
grow wiser and
become more sensitive and
are able to enjoy life more
after we go through
hard times
— Susan Polis Schutz

Realize that what you feel you lack in one regard may be more than compensated for in another. What you feel you lack in the present may become one of your strengths in the future. See your future filled with promise and possibility. Learn to view everything as a worthwhile experience.

— Sandra Sturtz Hauss

Difficult Times Don't Last Forever

Sometimes, the problems
you must face
are more than you wish
to cope with,
and tomorrow doesn't seem
to offer any solutions.

You may ask yourself "Why me?"
but the answer is sometimes unclear.
You may even tend to feel
that life hasn't been just or fair
to burden you with such obstacles.

The roads any of us choose
to follow are never free
of bumps or curves,
but eventually the turns
lead to a smoother path ahead.

Believe in yourself and your dreams.
You will soon realize that
the future holds many promises
for you.
Remember... difficult times
don't last forever.
— Geri Danks

You're in the Driver's Seat

Difficulties arise in the lives of us all. What is most important is dealing with the hard times, coping with the changes, and getting through to the other side where the sun is still shining just for you.

It takes a strong person to deal with tough times and difficult choices. But you are a strong person. It takes courage. But you possess the inner courage to see you through. It takes being an active participant in your life. But you are in the driver's seat, and you can determine the direction you want tomorrow to go in.

Hang in there... and take care to see that you don't lose sight of the one thing that is constant, beautiful, and true: everything will be fine — and it will turn out that way because of the special kind of person you are.

So... beginning today and lasting a lifetime through — hang in there, and don't be afraid to feel like the morning sun is shining... just for you.

— Douglas Pagels

Open Up
to Optimism

Optimism is the faith that leads to achievement;
nothing can be done without hope.

— Helen Keller

There is one thing which gives radiance to
everything: it is the idea of something around
the corner.

— G. K. Chesterton

Real optimism is aware of problems but recognizes the solutions, knows about difficulties but believes they can be overcome, sees the negatives but accentuates the positives, is exposed to the worst but expects the best, has reason to complain but chooses to smile.

— William Arthur Ward

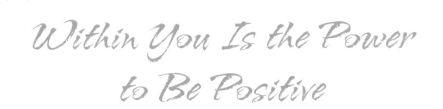

Within You Is the Power to Be Positive

If you are distressed by anything external, the pain is not due to the thing itself but to your own estimate of it; and this you have the power to revoke at any moment.

— Marcus Aurelius

This life is yours
Take the power
to choose what you want to do
and do it well
Take the power
to love what you want in life
and love it honestly
Take the power
to walk in the forest
and be a part of nature
Take the power
to control your own life
No one else can do it for you
Take the power
to make your life
healthy
exciting
worthwhile
and very happy

— Susan Polis Schutz

How to Be Happy

1. Make up your mind to be happy. Learn to find pleasure in simple things.

2. Make the best of your circumstances. No one has everything, and everyone has something of sorrow intermingled with gladness of life. The trick is to make the laughter outweigh the tears.

3. Don't take yourself too seriously. Don't think that somehow you should be protected from misfortune that befalls other people.

4. You can't please everybody. Don't let criticism worry you.

5. Don't let your neighbor set your standards. Be yourself.

6. Do the things you enjoy doing, but stay out of debt.

7. Never borrow trouble. Imaginary things are harder to bear than real ones.

8. Since hate poisons the soul, do not cherish jealousy, enmity, grudges. Avoid people who make you unhappy.

9. Have many interests. If you can't travel, read about new places.

10. Don't hold postmortems. Don't spend your time brooding over sorrows or mistakes. Don't be one who never gets over things.

11. Do what you can for those less fortunate than yourself.

12. Keep busy at something. A busy person never has time to be unhappy.

— Robert Louis Stevenson

Don't Dwell on
Your Troubles

Troubles are only mental; it is the mind that manufactures them, and the mind can gorge them, banish them, abolish them.

— Mark Twain

It is our attitude at the beginning of a difficult undertaking which, more than anything else, will determine its successful outcome.

— William James

Rather than wondering about or questioning the direction your life has taken, accept the fact that there is a path before you now. Shake off the "whys" and "what ifs," and rid yourself of confusion. Whatever was — is in the past. Whatever is — is what's important.

— Vicki Silvers

Drag your thoughts away from your troubles... it's the healthiest thing a body can do.

— Mark Twain

Enjoy the World Around You

The world was made
to be beautiful —
but sometimes we get caught up in
everyday actions
completely forgetting about this
completely forgetting that
what is truly important
are the simple, basic things in life —
honest, pure emotions
surrounded by the majestic beauty of nature
We need to concentrate on
the freeness and peacefulness of nature
and not on the driven material aspects of life
We need to smell the clear air
after the rainfall
and appreciate the good in things

Each of us must be responsible and do our part
in order to help preserve a beautiful world —
the waterfalls, the oceans, the mountains
the large gray boulders
the large green farms
the fluffy pink clouds
the sunrise and sunset, ladybugs
rainbows, dew, hummingbirds
butterflies, dandelions
We need to remember that
we are here for a short time
and that every day should count for something and
that every day we should be thankful
for all the natural beauty
The world is a wonderful place
and we are so lucky to be a part of it

— Susan Polis Schutz

Worrying Gets You Nowhere

Nothing wastes more energy than worrying.
The longer one carries a problem, the heavier it gets.
Don't take things too seriously.
Live a life of serenity, not a life of regrets.

— Douglas Pagels

The happiest people in the world are those who have
a hard time recalling their worries... and an easy
time remembering their blessings.

— Alin Austin

If you have occasional spells of despondency and self-pity, if once in a while you begin to feel sorry for yourself, don't despair! The sun has a sinking spell every night, but it rises again all right the next morning.

— Richard C. Hertz

Promise yourself to be so strong that nothing can disturb your peace of mind. To talk health, happiness, and prosperity to every person you meet. To look at the sunny side of everything and make your optimism come true. To think only of the best, to work only for the best, and to expect only the best. To forget the mistakes of the past and press on to the greater achievements of the future. To wear a cheerful countenance at all times and give every living creature you meet a smile.... To be too large for worry, too noble for anger, too strong for fear, and too happy to permit the presence of trouble.

— Christian D. Larson

Life is not measured by the number of breaths we take, but by the moments that take our breath away.

— Author Unknown

A positive attitude is contagious, but don't wait to catch it from others. Be a carrier.

— Author Unknown

Look for the Sun

There has not been a single day since the world began when the sun was not shining. The trouble has been with our vision.

— Author Unknown

Most of the shadows of this life are caused by standing in one's own sunshine.

— Ralph Waldo Emerson

A single sunbeam is enough to drive
away any shadows.

— Saint Francis of Assisi

Keep your face
    to the sunshine
and you cannot
    see the shadow.

— Helen Keller

Ten Thoughts to Help You Avoid Discouragement

1. Look at life as a journey, and enjoy the ride. Get the most out of the detours, and realize they're sometimes necessary.

2. Do your best, but if what you've been doing has caused you discouragement, try a different approach. Be passionate about the process, but don't be so attached to the outcome.

3. Wish the best for everyone, with no personal strings attached. Applaud someone else's win as much as you would your own.

4. Trust that there's a divine plan, that we don't always know what's best for us. A disappointment now could mean a victory later, so don't be disappointed. There is usually a reason.

5. Ask no more of yourself than the best that you can do, and be satisfied with that. Be compassionate toward yourself as well as others. Know your calling, your gift, and do it well.

6. Don't worry about something after it's done; it's out of your hands then, too late, over! Learn the lesson and move on.

7. Have the attitude that no one, except you, owes you anything. Give without expecting a thank-you in return. But when someone does something for you, be appreciative of even the smallest gesture.

8. Choose your thoughts or your thoughts will choose you; they will free you or keep you bound. Educate your spirit and give it authority over your feelings.

9. Judge no one, and disappointment and forgiveness won't be an issue. No one can let you down if you're not leaning on them. People can't hurt you unless you allow them to.

10. Love anyway... for no reason... and give... just because.

— Donna Fargo

Maintaining Optimism Is a Lifelong Process

Positive thinking is not the destination; it is the journey. An optimistic person will be constantly challenged — by external circumstances as well as inner fears and doubts. Always remember that these tests are like a ladder you must climb. As you move past each rung, your optimism strengthens and your confidence begins to flex newly found muscle that you might never have developed otherwise.

— Montague Edwards

Positive thinking is a habit, like any other;
we can practice it every day until it becomes
second nature to us — and along the way,
transform our lives.

— Washington L. Crowley

Always think on the bright side —
no matter what life brings
to your day.
You'll gain a treasure within your soul
that no worry or hardship
can ever take away.

— Isaac Purcell

Ten Ways to Make
Each of Your Days Positive

1. If each day is too short for all the wonderful things you want to do, don't be frustrated.

2. Be thankful... that your wish list is so full.

3. With the beginning of each sunrise, think to yourself: "Here's a brand-new day coming into my life. I can't wait to see how we'll get along! I wonder what's in store for us? What an adventure... spending time with a day I've never met before!"

4. Be open to the possibilities.

5. Count your blessings. Each one is so valuable, and they're the best treasures you've got. And while you're counting the big things, be sure to include the smaller ones, too.

6. A little added to a little... adds up to a lot.

7. Everyone's life is lived somewhere between their aspirations and their limitations. Successful people have limitations, like everyone else, and setbacks that are hard to ignore. But they offset them with efforts and aspirations... that absolutely soar.

8. Try hard and dream big.

9. If you think of your life as a story that gradually unfolds, you will embrace the changes and more fully appreciate the moments. You will know how natural it is for new chapters to begin and for the characters and events to surprise you every now and then. You will cherish your heroes and overcome your foes. And you can still have a beautiful story even if it hasn't been great all along. Make the best of everything, and...

10. Always enjoy reading the page you're on!

— Douglas Pagels

Positive Thinking Is...

...the key which unlocks the doors of the world. There is something in us which corresponds to that which is around us, beneath us, and above us.

— Samuel McChord Crothers

...knowing that, in the grand scheme of things, we live in a world where rainy days eventually give way to sunnier skies.

— R. L. Keith

...a constant attention to the details that make up an average day — with the knowledge that how you live this moment may reflect on the rest of your life.

— Jason Rogerson

...the ultimate triumph of mind over matter; the victory of the spirit over all the shadows lurking in the world.

— Martin A. Browning

...the most effective tool ever created for lifting an individual to the greatest achievements humanity can aspire to.

— Montague Edwards

Make Room in Your Life for These Things

Love — to shine like blue skies above you wherever you go, so you always know you're in the hearts of so many people.

Light — to see the end of the tunnel when you're struggling with troubles, so you always know you have the inner power to survive and triumph.

Laughter — to keep you healthy in mind and body; to give you the ability to act silly and exercise your giggle; to remind you that life is too short to be taken so seriously.

A lifeline in the form of family and friends —
to anchor you, support you, and keep you going
forward in a positive way when you're faced with
a crisis, so you always know you are a survivor.

Lots of positive thoughts — to help you fulfill all
your wishes, so you always know your possibilities
are unlimited... and success is your destiny.

— Jacqueline Schiff

Surround Yourself with Positive People

When someone cares
it is easier to speak
it is easier to listen
it is easier to play
it is easier to work

When someone cares
it is easier to laugh
— Susan Polis Schutz

Remember that a heart is like a garden that needs to be tended to and nourished with what only another heart can give — love and appreciation, devotion and honesty.

— Tracia Gloudemans

Guarantee your peace of mind, contentment, faith, and strength, as well as the constant ability to find joy in all the things that sometimes go unnoticed. Find moments to connect with other individuals who are full of smiles and hugs to give away and stories and laughter to share.

— Barbara Cage

The Power of Love

Love is the strongest and
   most fulfilling emotion possible
It lets you share your goals, your desires
   your experiences
It lets you share your life with someone
It lets you be yourself with someone
   who will always support you
It lets you speak your innermost feelings
   to someone who understands you
It lets you feel tenderness and warmth —
   a wholeness that avoids loneliness
Love lets you feel complete

— Susan Polis Schutz

Many people
go from one thing
to another
searching for happiness
But with each new venture
they find themselves
more confused
and less happy
until they discover
that what they are
searching for
is inside themselves
and what will make them happy
is sharing their real selves
with the ones they love

— Susan Polis Schutz

The Gift of a Smile

She smiled at a sorrowful stranger.
The smile seemed to make him feel better.
He remembered the past kindness of a friend
And wrote him a thank-you letter.
The friend was so pleased with the thank-you
That he left a large tip after lunch.
The waitress, surprised by the size of the tip,
Bet the whole thing on a hunch.
The next day she picked up her winnings,
And gave part to a man on the street.
The man on the street was grateful;
For two days he'd had nothing to eat.

After he finished his dinner,
He left for his small, dingy room.
He didn't know at that moment
That he might be facing his doom.
On the way he picked up a shivering puppy
And took him home to get warm.
The puppy was very grateful
To be in out of the storm.
That night the house caught on fire.
The puppy barked the alarm.
He barked till he woke the whole household
And saved everybody from harm.
One of the boys that he rescued
Grew up to be president.
All this because of a simple smile.

— Author Unknown

The Simple Act of Kindness

Drop a pebble in the water,
And its ripples reach out far;
And the sunbeams dancing on them
May reflect them to a star.

Give a smile to someone passing,
Thereby making his morning glad;
It may greet you in the evening
When your own heart may be sad.

Do a deed of simple kindness;
Though its end you may not see,
It may reach, like widening ripples,
Down a long eternity.

— Joseph Norris

Life is made up of little things —
in which smiles and kindnesses...
are what win and preserve the heart.

— Sir H. Davy

Kindness in words
    creates confidence.
Kindness in thinking
    creates profoundness.
Kindness in feeling
    creates love.

— Lao Tzu

Be Thankful for the Gifts You Receive Each Day

Look for something to be thankful
and glad over each day,
and you will find it....

Fill your soul and mind full of love
and sympathy and joy...
and blessings will follow.

— Ella Wheeler Wilcox

"Gratitude" is one of the nicest feelings a heart can have. It's a feeling that comes along for a very special reason — and it's a lovely thought that never goes away once it enters in. It joins together with precious memories and grateful hopes. Gratitude lives on, not for just a moment or a day, but through all the seasons that lie ahead.

— Marin McKay

When It's Hard to Be Positive...

Have hope. Because it works wonders for those who have it. Be optimistic. Because people who expect things to turn out for the best often set the stage to receive a beautiful result.

Count your blessings. Be inspired to climb your ladders and have some nice, long talks with your wishing stars. Be strong and patient, gentle and wise.

Believe in happy endings. Because you are the author of the story of your life.

— Douglas Pagels

Hope is not the closing of your eyes
    to the difficulty, the risk,
    or the failure.

It is a trust that — if I fail now —
    I shall not fail forever;
    and if I am hurt, I shall be healed.

It is a trust that life is good,
    love is powerful,
    and the future is full of promise.

— Author Unknown

Keep Things in Perspective

It's easy to look on the bright side of things when all is going well... when the smiles outweigh the frowns and the sunshine is streaming in the window.

But the happiest people are the ones who can say —
when all is going wrong, when the clouds get in
the way — that a little unhappiness must balance
the joys and that a bit of sadness has its place in
the world, too.

For these special people know of the balance of
nature's ways. They know that nothing grows
where the sun always shines and that gray skies
and rain can be an unregrettable sign of the day.

For these fortunate people, their favorite season
is always the one they are in, and they continue to
look on the bright side, knowing that the sunshine
might leave for a while, but that it will never be
gone for long.

— Jamie Delere

Sometimes We Need to Forgive and Start Over

Forgiveness is letting go of the pain
and accepting what has happened
because it will not change.

Forgiveness is dismissing the blame.
Choices were made that caused the hurt;
we each could have chosen differently,
but we didn't.

Forgiveness is looking at the pain,
learning the lessons it has produced,
and understanding what we have learned.

Forgiveness allows us to move on
toward a better understanding
of universal love
and our true purpose.

Forgiveness is knowing that love
is the answer to all questions
and that we all
are in some way connected.

Forgiveness is starting over
with the knowledge
that we have gained.
It is saying:
"I forgive you, and I forgive myself.
I hope you can do the same."

— Judith Mammay

This, Too, Shall Pass Away

When some great sorrow, like a mighty river,
   Flows through your life with peace-destroying power
And dearest things are swept from sight forever,
   Say to your heart each trying hour:
      "This, too, shall pass away."

When ceaseless toil has hushed your song of gladness
   And you have grown almost too tired to pray,
Let this truth banish from your heart its sadness
   And ease the burdens of each trying day:
      "This, too, shall pass away."

When fortune smiles and, full of mirth and pleasure,
　　The days are flitting by without a care,
Lest you should rest with only earthly treasure,
　　Let these few words their fullest import bear:
　　　　"This, too, shall pass away."

When earnest labor brings you fame and glory
　　And all earth's noblest ones upon you smile,
Remember that life's longest, grandest story
　　Fills but a moment in earth's little while:
　　　　"This, too, shall pass away."

　　　　　　　　　— Ella Wheeler Wilcox

Remember What Is Most Important...

It's not having everything go right;
it's facing whatever goes wrong.
It's not being without fear;
it's having the determination
    to go on in spite of it.

It's not where you stand,
but the direction you're going in.
It's more than never having bad moments;
it's knowing you are always
    bigger than the moment.

It's believing you have already
    been given everything
you need to handle life.
It's not being able to rid
    the world of all its injustices;
it's being able to rise above them.
It's the belief in your heart
    that there will always be
more good than bad in the world.
It's remembering that every day ends
and brings a new tomorrow
full of exciting new things.
It's loving what you do
and doing the best you can.

— Vickie M. Worsham

Live One Day at a Time

Each dawn is the beginning of a new life. Live life day by day to understand the joy that is in your heart.

— Louise Bradford Lowell

Having spent the better part of my life trying either to relive the past or experience the future before it arrives, I have come to believe that in between these two extremes is peace.

— Author Unknown

One day at a time — we have that ability, through cherishing each moment and rejoicing in each dream. We can experience each day anew, and with this fresh start, we have what it takes to make all our dreams come true. Each day is new, and living one day at a time enables us to truly enjoy life and live it to the fullest.

— Regina Hill

Take each day one at a time, and you'll be amazed at how your difficulties manage to become easier.

— Collin McCarty

Take Time To...

Lean against a tree
and dream your world of dreams
Work hard at what you like to do
and try to overcome all obstacles
Laugh at your mistakes
and praise yourself for learning from them
Pick some flowers
and appreciate the beauty of nature
Be honest with people
and enjoy the good in them

Don't be afraid to show your emotions
Laughing and crying make you feel better
Love your friends and family with your
    entire being
They are the most important part of your life
Feel the calmness on a quiet sunny day
and plan what you want to accomplish in life
Find a rainbow
and live your
world of dreams
                                    — Susan Polis Schutz

Picture a Positive Future

Life is like a giant puzzle.
Each of us has a picture
in our minds of how our lives will turn out.
We keep adding pieces, one at a time,
attempting to create that beautiful picture.
If one piece does not fit, we replace it
    with another.
We never get all the pieces in the right place
    on the first try.
It's all about experimenting until each piece
    fits together with the next.

Though our futures may not be clear
or turn out exactly as we expected,
each of us has the strength inside to put
the puzzle together.
We just have to look for the right pieces.
It may seem impossible, but keep striving.
Life's pieces have a way of falling into place
when you least expect it.

— Renée M. Brtalik

You Can Make Something Happy out of Everything That Happens in Life

Life can make choices for us.
Sometimes these choices
    seem unhappy or unfair,
but in the end we control
our own destiny because we can decide
    how people and events affect us.

So much of our happiness lies within
    the choices we make.
We can accept that life
    isn't the way we want it to be,
    or we can change it so that it will be.

We can walk through the shadows,
    or we can choose to smile
    and seek out the sunlight.
We can create grand dreams
    that never leave the ground,
    or we can be builders of dreams that come true.
We can look at only the negative aspects of ourselves,
    or we can lift ourselves up
    by being our own best friend.
We can live in the past
    or dream about the future,
    or we can live for today.
We can give up when the road becomes difficult,
    or we can keep on going
    until the view is much better.
The choices in life are endless,
    and so is the potential for happiness.

— Nancye Sims

Believe in Miracles!

Love your life.
Believe in your own power, your own potential,
    and your own innate goodness.
Every morning, wake with the awe of just being alive.
Each day, discover the magnificent, awesome beauty
    in the world.
Explore and embrace life in yourself and in everyone
    you see each day.
Reach within to find your own specialness.
Amaze yourself, and rouse those around you to the
    potential of each new day.

Don't be afraid to admit that you are less than perfect;
    this is the essence of your humanity.
Let those who love you help you.
Trust enough to be able to take.
Look with hope to the horizon of today, for today is all
    we truly have.
Live this day well.
Let a little sunshine out as well as in.
Create your own rainbows.
Be open to all your possibilities; possibilities can
    be miracles.
Believe in miracles!

— Vickie M. Worsham

Always Be
True to Yourself

Be true to the light that is deep within you. Hold
on to your joy for life. Keep good thoughts in your
mind and good feelings in your heart. Keep love
in your life, and you will find the love and light
in everyone.

Be giving, forgiving, patient, and kind. Have faith
in yourself. Be your own best friend, and listen to
the voice that tells you to be your best self.

Be true to yourself in the paths that you choose.
Follow your talents and passions; don't take the
roads others say you must follow because they
are the most popular. Take the paths where your
talents will thrive — the ones that will keep your
spirits alive with enthusiasm and everlasting joy.

Most of all, never forget that there is no brighter
light than the one within you. Keep on being true
to yourself. Keep shining your light on others
so they will have a reason to smile. Follow your
inner light to your own personal greatness, and
remember that you are admired and loved just
as you are.

— Jacqueline Schiff

Twelve Ways to Keep Smiling!

Hold on to your dreams, and never let them go * Show the rest of the world how wonderful you are! * Give circumstances a chance, and give others the benefit of the doubt * Wish on a star that shines in your sky * Take on your problems one by one and work things out * Rely on all the strength you have inside *

Let loose of the sparkle and spirit that you sometimes try to hide ✳ Stay in touch with those who touch your life with love ✳ Look on the bright side and don't let the losers keep you from winning ✳ Be yourself, because you are filled with special qualities that have brought you this far and that will always see you through ✳ Keep your spirits up ✳ Make your heart happy, and let it reflect on everything you do!

— Ceal Carson

A Positive Attitude Is Your Greatest Asset

Your living is determined not so much by what life brings to you as by the attitude you bring to life; not so much by what happens to you as by the way your mind looks at what happens.

Circumstances and situations do color life, but you have been given the mind to choose what the color will be.

— John Homer Miller

Go forward with your shoulders back, with your head high, and with a smile. With your enthusiastic spirit, perseverance, and integrity of character, put your intelligence, talents, and passion into action.

Never let setbacks excuse you from trying again. It often takes many attempts to be a success.

Never let negative people influence you or direct what you do. Always face forward and see your whole life shining bright for you. Never let go of your character, ideals, or activism for the good of this world.

Never let go of the passions that inspire you, guide you, and always smile on you. These passions will lead you to reach your fullest potential. Hold on to them, and they will keep you honest, caring, kind, and generous with the finest gifts your heart can give.

— Jacqueline Schiff

Let Your Positive Side Shine

Always hold honor as a high virtue. Despite how the world may be, rise above.

Always speak the truth, because others will hold you in high esteem as a person who can be trusted.

Never lose faith in your fellow human beings, despite times when they may let you down.

Believe in hard work. No one will hand you the future you want. The ladder to success is steep, but take one step at a time and you'll get to the top.

Always believe in yourself. Your happiness depends on no one else but you. If there is something that you are unhappy about, you must change it.

Always hold love close to you. When you make a commitment, cherish it for the rest of your life.

— Sherrie L. Householder

Make Every Day Special

Be thankful and look to every new day with positive hope.

Take time to pull yourself away from all the noise and just look around you. Take inventory. Appreciate those who have enhanced the quality of your life, and remember that they have been a gift to you. Also remember that you're a gift to them, too.

Be grateful for the choices you've made, both good and bad. Accept your mistakes; you can't change them anyway. Apply what you've learned and go on. Use these lessons to help you with your other decisions in life. Appreciate yourself and your own uniqueness.

Go outside and look at the sky. Soak in the atmosphere. Enjoy the colors of the landscape. Feel the textures of every place you are that you're thankful for. Smile at the world. Don't allow any negative feelings to creep into your consciousness. Feel the power of your own acceptance. Put a positive spin on every thought you have.

Make every day special. Own it. Enjoy it. Bask in the glory of life. Appreciate the gift of your own life.

— Donna Fargo

Carry These Gifts
with You Always...

Joy in your heart,
 your mind, your soul.
Peace with yourself
 and with the universe.
Harmony.
Courage to feel,
 to need, to reach out.

Freedom to let yourself
  be bound by love.
Friendship.
Wisdom to learn,
  to change, to let go.
Acceptance of the truth
  and beauty within yourself.
Growth.
Pleasure in all that you see
  and touch and do.
Happiness with yourself
  and with the world.
Love.
                    — Maureen Doan

Most of All... Be Happy!

Always see the goodness in this world,
do your part in helping those
    less fortunate,
walk hand in hand with those
    of less talent,
follow those of more knowledge,
and be an equal with those
    who are different.
Find your special purpose
    in this world so full of choices,
and help lead those who stray.
Become your own individual —
set yourself apart from those who
    are the same.

Have the self-confidence to say no
    when it is necessary
and the strength to stand alone.
Give yourself the approval to love and
    respect everything that you are
        and will become.
Reap the fruits of your talents,
walk with pride down the road of life,
be humble in your successes,
and share in the praises and joy of others.
Most of all, be happy.
For when you are happy,
    you have the key that will open all
        of the world's doors to you.

                                    — Jackie Olson

May You Always Have Positive Thoughts

May every day of your life bring you fresh hopes for tomorrow — because hope gives all of us our reason for trying. ☀ May each new day bring a feeling of excitement, joy, and a wonderful sense of expectation. Expect the best, and you'll get it. ☀ May you find peace in simple things, because those are the ones that will always be there.

May you remember the good times and forget the sorrow and pain, for the good times will remind you of how special your life has been. ✳ May you always feel secure and loved and know you are the best. ✳ May you experience all the good things in life — the happiness of realizing your dreams, the joy of feeling worthwhile, and the satisfaction of knowing you've succeeded. ✳ May you find warmth in others, expressions of love and kindness, smiles that encourage you, and friends who are loyal and honest. ✳ May you realize the importance of patience and accept others for what they are. With understanding and love, you'll find the good in every heart. ✳ May you have faith in others and the ability to be vulnerable. Open your heart and really share the miracle of love and intimacy. ✳ Above all, may you always have positive thoughts.

— Regina Hill

ACKNOWLEDGMENTS

We gratefully acknowledge the permission granted by the following authors and authors' representatives to reprint poems or excerpts from their publications.

Susan Polis Schutz for "Find happiness in nature…," "Keep in mind at all times…," "Positive Thinkers Have Twelve Qualities in Common," "Take Time To…," "Love is the strongest…," "Enjoy the World Around You," and "Do what you love…." Copyright © 1983, 1986, 1989, 1993, 2004 by Stephen Schutz and Susan Polis Schutz. And for "When someone cares…." Copyright 1976 by Continental Publications. Renewed © 2002 by Stephen Schutz and Susan Polis Schutz. And for "This life is yours" and "Many people go from one thing…." Copyright © 1979, 1980 by Continental Publications. All rights reserved.

PrimaDonna Entertainment Corp. for "Make Every Day Special," "Ten Thoughts to Help You Avoid Discouragement," and "Choose Your Thoughts Wisely" by Donna Fargo. Copyright © 1997, 2004, 2008 by PrimaDonna Entertainment Corp. All rights reserved.

A careful effort has been made to trace the ownership of selections used in this anthology in order to obtain permission to reprint copyrighted material and give proper credit to the copyright owners. If any error or omission has occurred, it is completely inadvertent, and we would like to make corrections in future editions provided that written notification is made to the publisher:

BLUE MOUNTAIN ARTS, INC., P.O. Box 4549, Boulder, Colorado 80306.